Kite Flying

Rhino on a Bike

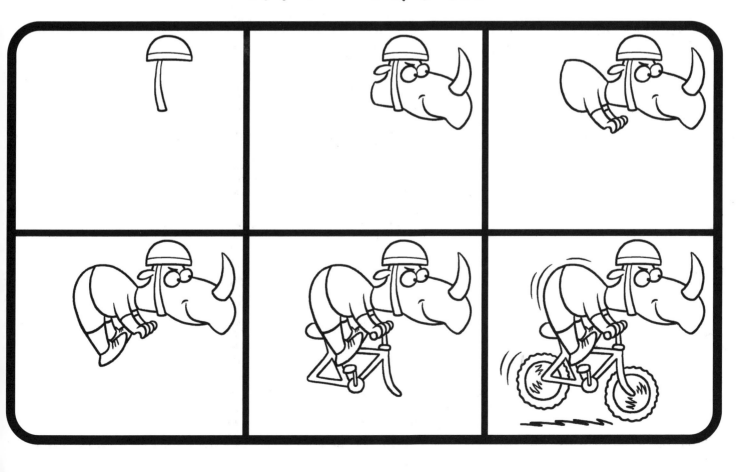

Shy Girl   # Surgeon

Body Builder

old Man

Freezing

Yo-yo Boy

Skating Bear

Reindeer

Crying Baby

Duck Spy

Knight on Horseback

Rock Drummer

Hiker

Space-hopper Girl

Teddy cuddle

Elephant Tightrope

Hungry Cat

Basketball Player

Surfing Shark

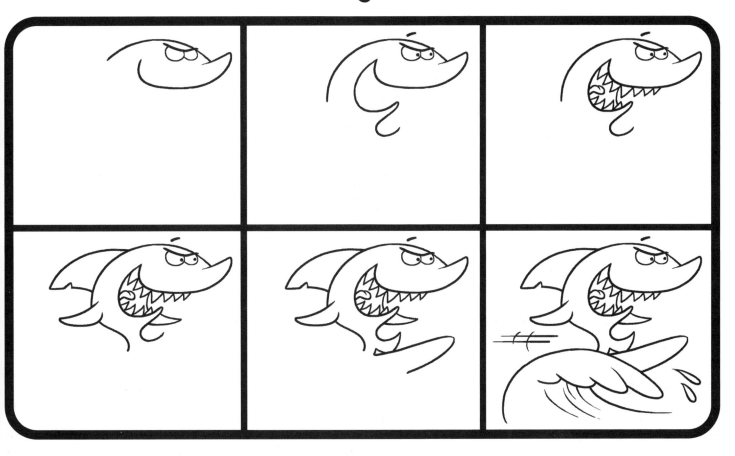

Speedy Snail

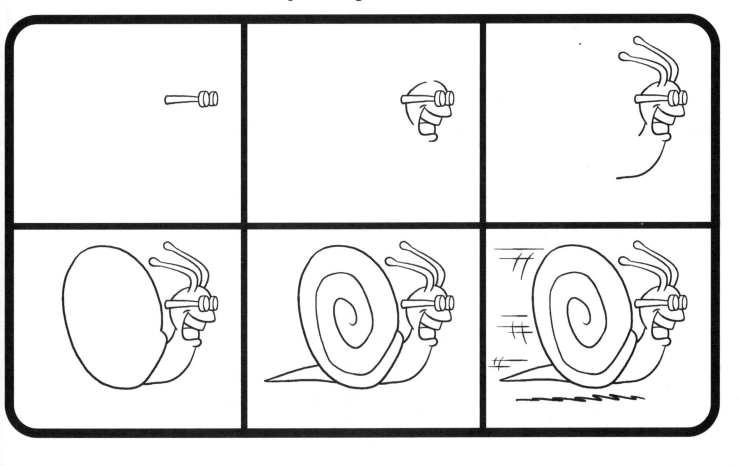

Keep-fit ostrich

Painter

frog Swimmer

Rock Star

Boy Scout

Pirate

Computer and Mouse

Tortoise

Cowboy

In Love

Viking

Wizard

Scientist

Witch

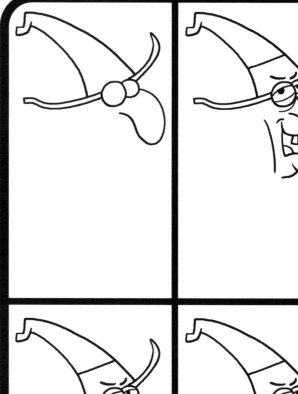

Goldfish Rave

Burglar

Santa

Cheeky Chicken

Champion

Little Angel

Little Devil

Busy Beaver

Queen

Punky Parrot

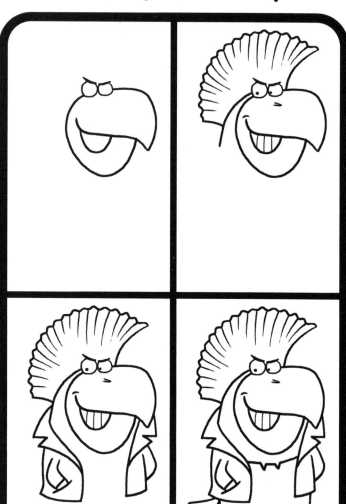

Bookworm

Sheila Sheep

Cool Banana

Silly Spider

Cell Phone

Hippy Hamster

Sherlock Bones